START-UP
ART AND DESIGN

MOTHER NATURE, DESIGNER

Louise and Richard Spilsbury

Cherrytree Books are distributed in the
United States by Black Rabbit Books
P.O. Box 3263
Mankato, MN, 56002

Library of Congress Cataloging-in-Publication Data

Spilsbury, Louise.
  Mother nature, designer / Louise and Richard
Spilsbury.
     p. cm. -- (Start-up art and design)
  Originally published: London : Evans, 2007.
  Includes index.
  "Explores the variety of patterns, shapes, colors, and
textures found in nature and encourages kids to use
nature as inspiration for their own projects. Includes
project ideas"--Provided by publisher.
  ISBN 978-1-84234-526-9
  1. Nature craft--Juvenile literature. 2. Nature in art--
Juvenile literature. I. Spilsbury, Richard, 1963- II. Title.

  TT157.S6745 2009
  738--dc22

                                                    2007046390

13-digit ISBN: 9781842345269
10-digit ISBN: 1842345265

First Edition
9 8 7 6 5 4 3 2 1

First published in 2007 by Evans Brothers Ltd.
2A Portman Mansions, Chiltern Street,
London W1U 6NR, United Kingdom

Produced for Evans Brothers Limited by
White-Thomson Publishing Ltd.

Copyright © Evans Brothers Limited 2007

Editor: Rachel Minay
Consultant: Susan Ogier Horwood
Designer: Leishman Design

Acknowledgments:

Special thanks to Ms. J. Arundell and pupils at Mayfield
Primary School, Hanwell, West London, for their help
and involvement in the preparation of this book.

Picture Acknowledgments:

Bridgeman Art Library p. 8t; Corbis pp. 13t (DLILLC),
16r (Christie's Images); Ecoscene p. 5bl; Evans Brothers
Ltd. p. 12t; Chris Fairclough pp. cover main, title page,
4l (inset), 6l&r, 7t&b, 8b, 9b, 10l, 11t, 13b, 17t&b, 18l&r,
19l&r, 21; iStockphoto.com pp. cover tl&r, 4l, 4r (both),
5tl,c&r, 5bc&r, 9t, 14 (all), 15r, 16l (all), 20 (all);
Shutterstock.com p. cover main (background).

Artwork:

Pupils at Mayfield Primary School, Hanwell, West
London pp. 12b, 15l; Amy Sparks pp. 10r, 11b.

Contents

Design in Nature

Nature is an amazing **designer**! There are many different shapes and patterns in nature.

"A spider's web has lines and circles that cross each other to make a net."

"Through my magnifying glass I can see the pattern of lines on these leaves."

designer   **magnifying**

▼ **Which habitats do these natural designs come from?**
Can you match the picture to the habitat?

Meadow   Pond   Woodland

Garden   Beach   Rock Pool

habitats

Investigating Nature

Jake's class investigates nature's designs. The children collect natural objects such as fallen leaves. They take photos of flowers and other living things.

"I'm using the zoom button to photograph details on plants."

"I'm making a record of the pattern of the bark."

Tip: Never collect living things and always wash your hands after touching natural objects.

► **The children make a nature display. What images have they used in their photos?**

"This is spiky, hard, and round. I think it's a chestnut in its case."

◄ **Some children make feely bags. Their friends describe the texture and shape of the objects inside and guess what they are.**

images   texture

Nature's Colors

In nature there are many shades of the same color. Henri Rousseau painted colorful jungles. Rousseau's paintings contain more than 50 shades of green!

◄ What sounds of nature would you hear if you were inside this painting?

► How many shades of green can you mix? Try mixing blues and yellows.

shades   jungles

▶ Fruits come in many colors and shapes. What would you use to create a **still life** picture of fruit? Would you choose paints, crayons, or **pastels**?

◀ **Zac is using watercolor pencils to draw the inside of an apple.**

"I'm adding water to the pencil marks to blend the colors."

still life   pastels   blend

Computer Creations

Create an exciting pattern using nature's designs and a computer.

◄ First use a **scanner** to make digital images of natural items such as flower heads and leave

► Use an **effects** tool on the computer to alter the colors of your scanned images. This can make the design more **unrealistic**.

scanner   effects   unrealistic

▲ You can also copy, rotate, and paste the images to create patterns.

► Which parts of this design are symmetrical?

rotate   paste   symmetrical

Animal Designs

▶ This book is about a girl and her blue dinosaur. Dinosaurs lived so long ago that we don't know what colors they really were.

Can you think of some colorful dinosaur designs? Write a poem about your fantasy dinosaur. Use lots of adjectives to describe it.

Mary had a Dinosaur

TWISTERS

Eileen Browne and Ruth Rivers

My dinosaur
　　My dinosaur is fat and bumpy.
　　　　She has sharp teeth and
　　　　　spiky sticks.
　　　　　　She has a long green tail
　　　　　　　and big black claws.
　　　　　　　　She looks out with her
　　　　　　　　　small yellow eye.

fantasy   adjectives   camouflage

Some animals use color to help them hide. This is called camouflage. Why do animals sometimes need to hide?

► Striped fur helps tigers hide in long grass.

You can copy and paste photographs of fur or feathers to make a patchwork pattern on the computer.

"I printed my patchwork on to transfer paper to put onto a T-shirt!"

Islamic Art

flower

citrus fruits

water ripples

Some of nature's designs form perfect geometric patterns. These remind Muslims of Allah's greatness.

Islamic art reflects nature's patterns. Twirling plants show nature's perfection. Circles do not end, which reminds Muslims that Allah is forever.

geometric   Muslims   Allah

Many Islamic buildings are decorated with beautiful geometric designs.

► This building is covered with patterned tiles.

You could paint a tile with a geometric pattern, or make a design for a tile on cardboard.

◄ Millie's class designed different tiles and put them together to make a colorful display.

Islamic   decorated

Bug Art

There are many beautiful insect designs, such as colorful butterfly wings. What other bug patterns can you think of?

► The artist who designed this glass lamp was inspired by insect patterns. How did the artist use symmetry in this lamp design?

insect   inspired

◀ **Emma is making bug art! First she draws a ladybug. Then she glues string over the outline to create a printing block.**

"I'm making a big cushion cover for the book corner."

▶ **She rolls the printing block with ink and prints the bug on to cloth. She repeats this to make a pattern.**

Nature Collage

Susie is making a nature collage that people can touch. She makes paper patterns for the main shapes.

"I use the paper patterns to cut out pieces of fabric."

Tip: Take care when using scissors.

"These beads will give a bumpy feel to the picture."

▶ Susie chooses materials to give her picture texture.

collage   fabric   materials

▼ Susie sews on the flower petals. What other methods can you use to join pieces together?

"My grandma can't see very well, but she'll be able to feel my picture."

What will you use to decorate your nature collage?

sews   methods

Thinking about Design

Nature inspires many kinds of designers.

▶ A bee's **honeycomb** is light but strong because it is made up of **hexagon** shapes.

▲ These buildings were inspired by honeycombs.

honeycomb   hexagon

Artists are often interviewed about their work.
In a role play, Zac is an interviewer.

"What inspired you to design this collage?"

"I got the idea from my garden at home."

If you were an interviewer, what questions would you ask?

Further Information for

New words listed in the text:

adjectives	display	images	materials	record	texture
Allah	effects	insect	methods	role play	transfer paper
blend	fabric	inspired	Muslims	rotate	unrealistic
camouflage	fantasy	interviewed	outline	scanner	
collage	geometric	investigates	paste	sews	
decorated	habitats	Islamic	pastels	shades	
designer	hexagon	jungles	patchwork	still life	
details	honeycomb	magnifying	printing block	symmetrical	

Possible Activities

PAGES 4-5

Children can collect and look at details of nature's designs using a magnifying glass or, in class, a microscope.

We identify trees by their leaf shape. There is a page of different leaf shapes at
http://www.teachingkate.org/lessons/pendleton.pdf.

Pupils could look at examples of natural objects, both real and pictures they find in books or magazines. They could then make detailed drawings of these. Discuss the lines and shapes in the pupils' drawings and identify the different features.

PAGES 6-7

Children could label a display of found natural objects to inspire visitors to think about texture, with questions such as "Which is the roughest object here?" They could also make and include 3D mobiles of some of their found objects.

As well as rubbings and photos, children can take imprints of objects (such as cones) in clay or make sketches of interesting natural designs. They could describe the lines and patterns in the design, e.g. wiggly, spotted.

PAGES 8-9

Work on nature's colors links with the changing colors of the seasons. Children could make a four-part poster showing one natural scene and the way its colors change throughout the seasons. Work on fruit can link to healthy eating and to science, for example finding out why fruits have seeds inside.

The Family Zone of the Tate Modern has a section on Rousseau at http://www.tate.org.uk/modern/exhibitions/rousseau.

PAGES 10-11

The children could scan in a flower head and then create a heavily pixelated version of its digital image and print it out in sections. They can then make a mosaic image with the pieces. See http://www.ncaction.org.uk/search/item.htm?id=1373.

If you do not have a scanner, there are digital images of nature photos and close-ups of natural objects such as flowers at http://www.theimagegallery.co.uk/p_macro.htm, which children could use to create patterns on the computer.

PAGES 12-13

To learn more about animals and their habitats, children could look at other animal patterns and colors and think about how

Parents and Teachers

they use color. As well as camouflage, color can be used to send signals, to warn other animals, or to attract animals. The book shown is *Mary Had a Dinosaur* by Eileen Browne (ISBN: 978 0 23753 341 0, Evans Publishing Group).

PAGES 14-15

To study alternative cultures that use nature in their art, children could research African masks and then make one of their own. They could also discuss examples of Aboriginal art. See http://www.aboriginalartonline.com/index.php

PAGES 16-17

Children could do an Art Nouveau tissue window (pieces of colored tissue stuck over holes in cardboard) with nature designs to emulate Tiffany glass, or make tissue paper flowers. To expand textiles work, the children could look at William Morris. You can view Morris designs and also download wallpaper patterns at http://www1.walthamforest.gov.uk/wmg/home.htm. The children could make a Morris-inspired sheet of wallpaper.

PAGES 18-19

Children could look at Matisse's paper cutouts to help them simplify shapes and to think of ways of making more abstract designs. When making an appliqué picture or collage, children could look at ways of preparing the materials they use, such as pleating, scrunching, and folding, before they sew, glue, pin, or staple them on.

PAGES 20-21

Looking at how nature influences designers provides good links with science. The picture shows the Eden Project in Cornwall, England. Children could also look at the hexagonal shapes of the facets in an insect's compound eye. Other designs inspired by nature include Velcro (from plant burrs) and reflectors in the road.

Interviewing each other in a role such as an art critic or interviewer gives the children the chance to comment on each other's work more openly and is a fun drama activity. Some children could record the interview and play it back on the computer or TV.

Further Information

BOOKS FOR CHILDREN

Paper Flowers (Usborne How to Guides) by Ray Gibson (Usborne Publishing Ltd, 1995)

Insects, Bugs, & Art Activities (Arty Facts) by Polly Goodman and Steve Parker (Crabtree Publishing Company, 2002)

Animals & Art Activities (Arty Facts) by Janet Sacks (Crabtree Publishing Company, 2002)

Nature Crafts (Creative Kids) by Joy Williams (North Light Books, 2002)

Nature's Art Box: From T-Shirts to Twig Baskets, 65 Cool Projects for Crafty Kids to Make with Natural Materials You Can Find Anywhere by Laura C. Martin (Storey Publishing, 2003)

WEB SITES

www.kinderart.com/painting/

http://susieshort.net/watercolor-tips.html

www.artsconnected.org/classroom/

www.nature-inspired.org

www.drawingpower.org.uk

www.tate.org.uk/learning/kids

Index